Hidden Thoughts and Emotions

Erica Teagle

BookLeaf Publishing

India | USA | UK

Presentation by *BookLeaf Publishing*

Web: www.bookleafpub.com

E-mail: info@bookleafpub.com

ISBN: 9789363303713

First edition 2024

ACKNOWLEDGEMENT

I would like to thank God for giving me this opportunity to share my thoughts and emotions in this work of art. I thank the people that have been and are in my life for their roles, lessons, and shared memories. I would like to thank my friend, Memo, who has helped and encouraged me through this process. I'm truly grateful.

PREFACE

"No matter what happens, or how bad it seems today. Life does go on and it will be better tomorrow." - Maya Angelou

Lil' Rick

Into the night, I drove back home with my
thoughts filled with you.
Tears rolled down my face as I looked back.
If I'd known our embrace was the last, I would
have never let you go.
I would have said the things that I wanted to say.
I would have stayed longer to hear your wisdom.
The thought that we would grow old together is
now a dream.
For that September you took His hand, and said,
"Goodbye."
Now, the only place I can see you is in the sky.

Unspoken Words to Mom

Mom, I grew up watching and admiring you, yet not understanding you.
As an adult, I now know that you were a person with broken pieces that needed to heal while doing your best.

Mom, I wish our roles were reversed, with me as the mother and you as the child. I would brush your hair without your tears. I would ask you about your day, and then afterwards, we could play.

Mom, I would tell you that you're beautiful with your hazel eyes, and that your dreams are as limitless as the sky. I would talk to you gently, not yell. I would pick you up and not bring you down.

Mom, I would hold you close and not push you away. I would give you the love and stability you desired, if you were my child.

Victorious

You were once a stranger to me, but as I grew up, you followed me closely. You even became chained to me and started weighing me down. Oh, how you cause me to pace back and forth while turning my stomach into knots. You even invited your companion, Doubt, to whisper sweet words in my ear of defeat and fear. Now, you both watch and chuckle at my struggles. Anxiety and Doubt, I've grown tired of these games. Today, I stand before you both with determination to be victorious. You may win the battle, but not the war.

Time

Time doesn't wait for anyone. I remember eagerly counting down the years until I was an adult. I blinked, and now I'm grown. It's ironic that I wish the hands of time would return to when I was small. Back to the simpler days without a care in the world.

Being Positive

You all say that I'm always laughing and grinning. That I'm like sunshine. I've succeeded in showing you all my best. But it's a struggle to not let my inner demons get the best of me. On the days that I lose, I shed tears in private and stifle my cries. It's hard to be positive. Being positive is a daily choice that I try to make in this already negative world.

Love

Love is many things that reveal itself in different forms: romance, friendship, kindness, and honesty, to name a few.

Love comes from a place of good intent. When I hear others say, "Love isn't so." I want to ask them, "Why?" I want to tell them that the love they experienced was something else in disguise. Because love accepts the good and the bad. Love is a choice. Love is an action.

Men and Women

The saying, "Men are from Mars and women are from Venus," indeed holds some truth. How men and women express emotions are different. But at the end of the day, they both are human beings. In today's hook-up culture, it's saddening that men and women have to wear masks. Men and women cannot waive their white flags and remove their armor to show their vulnerabilities. To show each other their desire to love and to be loved.

Thalia and Melpomene

The world seems to be more bitter than kind. We are living in a world where our interactions are short and superficial, rather than genuine. Society's expectations are fueled by stereotypes of creed and class, normalizing people to wear the face of Thalia when life throws a curve. There's nothing wrong with showing the face of Melpomene; it doesn't make you weak. It just shows that you're only human.

Heartbreak

I knew the end was near when you'd said, "You needed some time to yourself." I tried to brace myself for the words and the heartbreak, but I could never have been prepared for the emotions that hit me like waves. I mourned as I saw the plans that we'd made together go up in flames. And I, too, was consumed. Deep down, I knew you had served a purpose. As time passed, I prayed that I would rise like a phoenix.

Begin Again

Starting over often looks like a clean slate, or a reintroduction to the familiar, yet unknown. Going back to what's familiar can bring comfort, but at the same time, it brings anxiety knowing that old wounds will resurface with encounters. What's unknown is how the made plans and relationships will follow. I've learned that sometimes the best plans are the ones that are unplanned and unexpected.

Acceptance

"You have beautiful skin."
I have flawed skin.

"You're beautiful."
I have days where I don't feel beautiful;
I just look okay.

I have days when I look in the mirror and don't like what I see. I critique my appearance and internal state. Acceptance is a hard trait to incorporate because it involves loving both the parts of yourself that you show to the world, as well as the self that you lock away. I must remember to give myself grace and love while straightening my crown.

Healing

Healing is a process that is uncomfortable. It forces you to sit with yourself in a state of discomfort. The tests in life confirm one's state through events and people that reflect old scars. I have had moments where I thought I was over the past, only to react in that moment as if it had happened for the first time. I have to remind myself that I'm in the present. Healing is a non-linear process that doesn't have a set date. But a set goal. It has the goal of progressing to become a better person with patience each day.

Friendship

Through the seasons of my life, people have come and gone. But you are one of the few who have remained the same. Despite our distance and few talks, our hearts remain close. I treasure the time, joy, and relationship that we have. For what I have with you is rare. I'm blessed to call you my dearest friend.

First Love

It's true when they say, "You don't forget your first love." And you said it too. Our relationship was far from perfect, but we gave it our best. Despite the heartache, I did not hate you. Instead, I thanked you. I thanked you for our time together. I thanked you for pushing me past my comfort zone as a sign of growth. I thanked you for teaching me what I needed to experience in order to learn. We may not be on the same path, but it still remains true what I said to you that day, "I truly wish you the best."

Inner Child

I see glimpses of a little girl with a smile on her face when she's at an amusement park, or on the swings. Her laughter fills the air. Other times, I see this little girl in darkness. She is chained by her experiences and words of the past. She looks up, and I realize that she's me. I hold her close, and tell her that she's safe. I assure her that things are different this time. I ask, "Are you ready to heal?" She says, "Yes, but it's scary." I reply, "You're not alone."

Second Chance

Since coming back home, past events have been repeating themselves. They are presenting opportunities that I'd missed or didn't appreciate when they were first given. I look at my family with the thought that I have been given a second chance to cherish the little things, and fundamental ideals of family that I should have been endowed with. I'm relearning. I'm blessed to have had God pick them as my teachers and safe space.

Future Husband

Dear Future Husband,
I can't wait to meet you, even though I haven't laid my eyes on you, nor heard your voice. As I wait patiently for that day to come, I hope you will be a man who accepts my quirks and flaws with a smile. You give love and patience to the me that you see, and to the little girl inside. What lies ahead will not be easy; there will be times of highs and lows. When we falter, let us rely on each other, talk to each other, and pray together. Future husband, as we grow old together, I hope we become more child-like so that we never lose our sense of humor and bond. Future husband, I can't wait to go through this thing called life with you.

What Are You?

What are you?
I'm a Black woman.
What are you?
I'm a daughter, a sister, a niece, an aunt, and a
friend.
What are you?
I'm a person who's healing.
What are you?
I'm someone who's perfectly imperfect.
What are you?
I'm *me*—the good, the bad, and everything in
between.